Mother's Day Gift Book

by Ralph Lane

Thank you for selecting a Ralph Lane book. Ralph's gift books make great presents for birthdays, holidays, gift baskets, stocking stuffers, bathroom books, vacation books or just for the fun of it. Please consider leaving a review for this book on amazon.com or goodreads.com. And don't forget to suggest these fine Ralph Lane books to your friends and family:

Dad Jokes Gift Book

Dad Jokes Christmas Gift Book

Dad Jokes Valentine's Day Gift Book

Dad Jokes St. Patrick's Day Gift Book

Dad Jokes Easter Gift Book

Table of Contents

Riddle Me This Mom --------------------1

Fun Quotes For Mom ------------------5

Inspirational Quotes For Mom --------6

Mother's Day Timeline -----------------9

Famous Moms Throughout History --10

Poems For Mother --------------------13

Puzzlers for Mom ---------------------19

Mother's Day Trivia -------------------22

Answers to Riddles & Puzzles--------23

Riddle Me This Mom

(Answers on page 23 - 24)

1. Two mothers and two daughters went out to eat. Everyone ate one burger, yet only three burgers were eaten in all. How is this possible?

2. What word begins and ends with an E but only has one letter?

3. What type of cheese is made backwards?

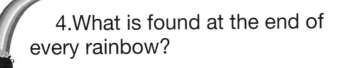

4. What is found at the end of every rainbow?

5. What goes up but never comes down?

6. What starts with the letter "T," is filled with "T," and ends in "T?"

7. A girl is sitting in a house at night with no lights on at all. There is no lamp, no candle, nothing. Yet she is reading. How?

8. What gets wetter and wetter the more it dries?

9. Name four days of the week that start with the letter "T."

10. What appears once in a minute, twice in a moment, but never in a thousand years?

11. A cowgirl rode into town on Friday, stayed for three days, then left on Friday. How did she do it?

12. You look out on a lake and see a boat full of people, yet there isn't a single person on board. How is that possible?

13. If there are three apples and you take away two, how many do you have?

14. How is Europe like a frying pan?

15. Beth's mother has three daughters. One is called Laura, the other one is Sarah. What is the name of the third daughter?

16. Why are ghost children bad liars?

17. What do the numbers 11, 69, and 88 all have in common?

18. What word looks the same backwards and upside down?

19. A girl fell off a 20-foot ladder but did not get hurt. Why not?

20. What five-letter word becomes shorter when you add two letters to it?

21. Imagine you're in a room that is filling with water. There are no windows or doors. How do you get out?

22. What futuristic invention lets you look right through a wall?

23. I can get a hundred feet in the air while I'm still touching the ground. What am I?

24. What are the two strongest days of the week?

25. What are two delicious things you can't have for breakfast?

26. What has one horn and complains all the time? (More of a joke than a riddle, but you'll love both answers.)

Fun Quotes For Mom

"My mother's menu consisted of two choices: Take it or leave it." - Buddy Hackett

"I want my children to have all the things I couldn't afford. Then I want to move in with them." - Phyllis Diller

"All women become like their mothers. That is their tragedy. No man does. That's his." - Oscar Wilde

"Children are gleeful barbarians." - Joseph Morgenstern

"We spend the first twelve months of our children's lives teaching them to walk and talk and the next twelve telling them to sit down and shut up." - Phyllis Diller

Inspirational Quotes For Mom

 "To a child's ear, '*mother*' is magic in any language." - Arlene Benedict

"There is no way to be a perfect mother, and a million ways to be a good one" - Jill Churchill

"Biology is the least of what makes someone a mother." - Oprah Winfrey

"When you are a mother, you are never really alone in your thoughts. A mother always has to think twice, once for herself and once for her child." – Sophia Loren

"The hand that rocks the cradle is the hand that rules the world."- W.R. Wallace

"A mother's love is patient and forgiving when all others are forsaking, it never fails or falters, even though the heart is breaking"- Helen Rice

"A mother is the truest friend we have…"- Washington Irving

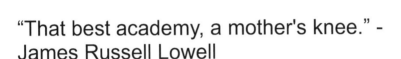

"The phrase 'working mother' is redundant." - Jane Sellman

"That best academy, a mother's knee." - James Russell Lowell

"A little girl, asked where her home was, replied, '*Where mother is*.'" - Keith L. Brooks

"A mother is one to whom you hurry when you are troubled." - Emily Dickinson

"The moment a child is born, the mother is also born. She never existed before. The woman existed, but the mother, never. A mother is something absolutely new." - Rajneesh

"All that I am or ever hope to be, I owe to my angel Mother." - Abraham Lincoln

 "Making the decision to have a child - It's momentous. It is to decide forever to have your heart go walking around outside your body."- Elizabeth Stone

"God could not be everywhere, so he created mothers." - Jewish Proverb

"My mother was an angel upon earth. She was a minister of blessing to all human beings within her sphere of action. Her heart was the abode of heavenly purity... She was the real personification of female virtue, of piety, of charity, of ever active and never intermitting benevolence." - Quincy Adams

"My mother was the making of me. She was so true, so sure of me; and I felt I had something to live for, someone I must not disappoint." -Thomas Alva Edison

"Every education begins with Mama." - Waris Dirie

Mother's Day Timeline

year or era	event
BCE	Motherhood has been celebrated in one form or another for at least the last two millennia but probably much longer than that. The Romans and Greeks held festivals to honor the Mother Goddesses Rhea and Cybele.
16th century	An early Christian festival known as Mothering Sunday may be the first celebration that was somewhat similar to what we now call Mother's Day although it began more to honor the 'mother church.'
mid 19th century just prior to Civil War	After most of her babies died of diseases (only four of her possibly 13 children survived to adulthood) **Ann Jarvis** wanted to help other mothers. She organized *Mothers' Day Work Clubs* in what is now West Virginia to help provide medical care, raise money for medicines, and improve sanitary conditions for poor mothers.
1868	**Ann Jarvis** started 'Mothers' Friendship Day' which was designed to promote reconciliation between Union and Confederate soldiers.
1870	**Julia Ward Howe**, writer of *Battle Hymn of the Republic*, combined her interests in suffrage and pacifism and wrote an *Appeal to Womanhood throughout the World*. Also called the *Mother's Day Proclamation*, the appeal urged women to come together to support peace. She had six children but made time to write essays and organize rallies for an annual Mother's Day for Peace.
1873	**Julia Ward Howe** lobbied for a *Mother's Peace Day* to be celebrated on the second of June each year.
1908	**Anna Jarvis**, daughter of Ann Jarvis, organized the first Mother's Day celebration at a church in Grafton, West Virginia.
1912	Numerous churches, towns and states begin to unofficially adopt Mother's Day as an annual holiday.
1914	Thanks to the ongoing efforts of **Anna Jarvis**, President **Woodrow Wilson** signed an official measure that establised the second Sunday in May as Mother's Day.

Famous Moms Throughout History

Marie Curie was the first woman to win a <u>Nobel Prize</u>. she raised her two young daughters alone after her husband died in an accident in 1906.

Sojourner Truth escaped slavery, with her baby daughter. Soon after her escape, she raised money for a lawyer, filed a complaint in court and successfully got her son out of slavery also. She went on to become a preacher and toured the northeast, speaking about the Bible, abolition, and women's suffrage.

Abigail Adams was the second First Lady of the United States who often single-handedly ran the family farm, wrote letters supporting equal rights for women, advocated for the abolition of slavery and educated their five kids including one who became a U.S. President.

Kathy Headlee was the mother of seven who started *Mothers Without Borders* to help orphaned children around the world.

Candy Lightner was the founder of Mothers Against Drunk Driving (MADD) to try to end drunk driving, pass tougher legislation and help the victims of drunk drivers.

Waris Dirie was a five year old victim of female genital mutilation in Somalia. Then, at thirteen, her parents arranged for her to marry a man in his sixties. She ran away to London. She became a successful model and actress then retired and founded an organization called *Desert Flower* that combats female genital mutilation around the world.

Indira Gandhi was India's first female Prime Minister and mother of two children who both grew up to become politicians. Her son, Rajiv, became Prime Minister of India after his mother was assassinated in 1984.

Dr. Dana Suskind was a widowed mother of three and a pediatric surgeon at the University of Chicago who founded the *Thirty Million Words Initiative* to encourage parents to talk frequently to their babies.

Mary Kay Ash was a single mom of three children. She also worked in sales at a home products company. She was repeatedly passed over for promotions despite her being one of the top sales directors. In 1963, at the age of 45, she founded what would become a billion-dollar cosmetics company that bore her name.

Poems For Mother

if there are any heavens my mother
will(all by herself)
     have
    one.   It will not be a pansy
heaven nor
    a fragile heaven of lilies-of-the-
valley but
    it will be a heaven of blackred
roses

    —from "if there are any heavens
my mother will(all by
      herself)have"

—by E.E. Cummings

Green sap of Spring in the young wood-
a-stir
    Will celebrate the Mountain Mother,
And every song-bird
        shout awhile for her

**—from "The White Goddess" by
Robert Graves**

My mother would be a falconress,
    and I her gerfalcon raised at her will,
    from her wrist sent flying, as if I were
her own
    pride, as if her pride
    knew no limits, as if her mind
    sought in me flight beyond the
horizon.

**—from "My Mother Would Be a
Falconress" by Robert Duncan**

Like those old pear-shaped Russian
dolls that open
    at the middle to reveal another and
another, down
    to the pea-sized, irreducible minim,
    may we carry our mothers forth in
our bellies.

**—from "The Envelope" by Maxine
Kumin**

I lie here now as I once lay
    in the crook of her arm, her creature,
    and I feel her looking down onto me
the way the
    maker of a sword gazes at his face in
the
    steel of the blade

**—from "Why My Mother Made Me"
by Sharon Olds**

I am a tree
  Strong limbed and deeply rooted
  My fruit is bittersweet
  I am your mother

—from "Trees" by Walter Dean Myers

The angels, whispering to one another,
  Can find, among their burning terms
of love,
  None so devotional as that of
"Mother"...

**—from "To My Mother" by Edgar
Allan Poe**

Today I remember
  The creator,
  The lion-hearted.

**—from "For My Mother" by May
Sarton**

And may you happy live,
And long us bless;
Receiving as you give
Great happiness.

**—from "To My Mother" by
Christina Rossetti**

To her whose heart is my heart's quiet
home,
To my first Love, my Mother, on
whose knee
I learnt love-lore that is not
troublesome;
Whose service is my special dignity,

**—from "Sonnets are full of love, and
this my tome" by Christina Rossetti**

Ah to sing the song of you, my matron
mighty!
My sacred one, my mother.

**—from "Delicate Cluster" by Walt
Whitman**

Ma, hear me now, tell me your story
   again and again.

**—from "From a Heart of Rice
Straw" by Nellie Wong**

If I were damned of body and soul,
   I know whose prayers would make
me whole...

**—from "Mother o' Mine" by
Rudyard Kipling**

My mother dandled me and sang,
   'How young it is, how young!'
   And made a golden cradle
   That on a willow swung.

**—from "The Player Queen" by W.
B. Yeats**

Puzzlers for Mom

(Answers found on page 25.)

Crossword for Mom

(But never a cross word from Mom)

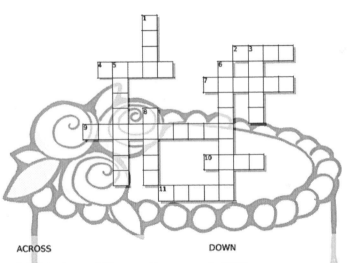

ACROSS

2 Mama always said there would be _____ like this.

4 Look Ma, no _____.

7 Mother's little _____

9 "Mama always said life is like a box of _____."

10 Do you _____ your mother with that mouth?

11 My mama didn't raise no _____.

DOWN

1 Mama _____ me not to come.

3 _____ pie and motherhood

5 Kid tested, mother _____.

6 _____ is the mother of all invention.

8 _____ thy father and mother.

19

Find all the Mom-related words or phrases in the following word search puzzle. Most of them are words that can be placed right before or after the words *Mother, Mama* or *Mom*. All the hidden words are located in the column to the right of the puzzle. To make this word search more difficult, cover the words on your first attempt. The answers to this puzzle are on page 26.

The Mother of All Word Searches

R	G	T	B	C	M	A	T	R	I	A	R	C	H
E	E	T	I	M	U	O	A	N	D	P	O	P	E
M	S	O	I	S	N	T	C	R	E	C	C	O	S
A	U	O	P	G	C	M	M	A	O	M	P	R	S
E	O	P	U	E	E	A	O	M	R	O	R	P	C
A	H	E	I	M	M	R	T	M	R	M	O	S	S
E	A	Y	I	U	E	O	H	O	O	M	E	B	S
A	Y	O	M	M	M	H	E	M	S	Y	M	U	E
Y	A	O	P	I	H	S	R	R	B	Y	P	A	I
N	T	I	B	A	P	G	S	M	R	E	I	H	O
H	T	R	A	E	G	U	D	R	R	M	A	S	E
K	N	A	T	U	R	E	A	O	K	T	R	L
I	T	H	O	C	K	E	Y	A	O	O	L	H	S
A	U	H	E	L	I	C	O	P	T	E	R	O	R

MIA
TONGUE
BEAR
MOMMA
MOTHERS DAY
HOUSE
TIGER
HELICOPTER
HOCKEY
SOCCER
SHIP
MOMMY
AND POP
BOY
SUPER
EARTH
MATRIARCH
MUM
NATURE

20

See how many of the following motherly song lyrics you recognize and then try matching the lyrics with the artists who performed them. You can either draw a line between the correct matches or write the letter of the corresponding artist to the right of the appropriate lyric. (Answers found on page 27.)

Song Lyrics Just For Mom

1. Stacy's mom has got it going on.

2. Mama, I love you, Mama I care.

3. If daddy had only seen...mommy kissing Santa Claus last night!

4. Hey Mama, I wanna scream so loud for you...Cuz' I'm so proud of you!

5. Mama don't cry no more... better days are there for sure.

6. I want a mom that will last forever; I want a mom who will love me whatever.

7. Cuz' mom you were always there...the perfect fan.

8. Momma, all you had to offer was the promise of a lifetime of love.

9. Mom, her face is still the same, she never seems to change, her love will still remain.

10. Mamma, Thank you for who I am.

11. Mamma, woo-oo-oo-oo; didn't mean to make you cry.

12. So, mother, I thank you, for all you've done and still do.

13. Ain't nobody got a mom like mine.

A. Earth, Wind and Fire

B. Gyptian

C. Fountain's of Wayne

D. The Spice Girls

E. Backstreet Boys

F. Christina Aguilera

G. Cindy Lauper

H. Jimmy Boyd

I. Kanye West

J. Il Divo

K. Celine Dion

L. Queen

M. Meghan Trainor

Mother's Day Trivia

Many cultures and countries set aside a day to recognize the tremendous impact Moms make on families and societies. However, there's no consensus on the actual date, so a version of Mother's Day occurs at different times around the world... just a few examples:

- U.S. and Canada: second Sunday in May
- UK: fourth Sunday in Lent
- Norway: second Sunday in February
- Egypt: first day of Spring - March 21
- Thailand: August 12
- Russia: last Sunday in November

- Most Kids: Mrs. Vassilyev of Russia gave birth to 69 children between 1725 and 1765.

- Oldest Mom: Rosanna Dalla Corte gave birth to a baby boy when she was 63 years old in Italy in 1994.

- Heaviest Newborn: Signora Carmelina Fedele gave birth to a 22 lb 8 oz boy in Italy in 1955.

Answers to Riddles & Puzzles

(Here are the answers to the riddles from pages 1 -4.)

1. They were a grandmother, mother, and daughter.

2. Envelope

3. Edam

4. The letter W

5. Your age

6. A teapot

7. She is blind and reading Braille.

8. A towel

9. Tuesday, Thursday, today, and tomorrow

10. The letter M

11. Her horse's name is Friday.

12. All the people on the boat are married.

13. If you take two apples, then you have two.

14. Because it has Greece at the bottom.

15. Beth

16. Because their mother can see right through them.

17. They read the same right side up and upside down.

18. SWIMS

19. She fell off the bottom step.

20. Short

21. Stop imagining.

22. A window

23. A centipede lying on its back

24. Saturday and Sunday (The rest are weekdays.)

25. Lunch and dinner

26. A WHINEoceros (or a teenage unicorn)

Answer key for crossword puzzle from page 19

Crossword for Mom
(But never a cross word from Mom)

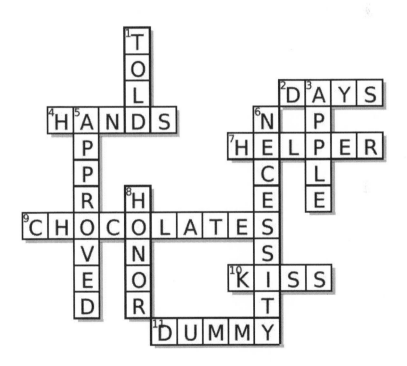

Answer key for *Mother of All Word Searches* puzzle on page 20

The Mother of All Word Searches

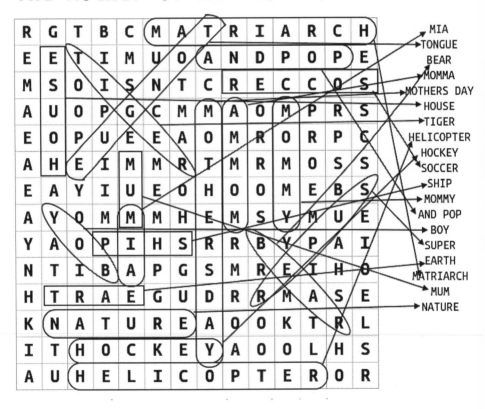

R	G	T	B	C	M	A	T	R	I	A	R	C	H
E	E	T	I	M	U	O	A	N	D	P	O	P	E
M	S	O	I	S	N	T	C	R	E	C	C	O	S
A	U	O	P	G	C	M	M	A	O	M	P	R	S
E	O	P	U	E	E	A	O	M	R	O	R	P	C
A	H	E	I	M	M	R	T	M	R	M	O	S	S
E	A	Y	I	U	E	O	H	O	O	M	E	B	S
A	Y	O	M	M	M	H	E	M	S	Y	M	U	E
Y	A	O	P	I	H	S	R	R	B	Y	P	A	I
N	T	I	B	A	P	G	S	M	R	E	I	H	O
H	T	R	A	E	G	U	D	R	R	M	A	S	E
K	N	A	T	U	R	E	A	O	K	T	R	L
I	T	H	O	C	K	E	Y	A	O	O	L	H	S
A	U	H	E	L	I	C	O	P	T	E	R	O	R

MIA
TONGUE
BEAR
MOMMA
MOTHERS DAY
HOUSE
TIGER
HELICOPTER
HOCKEY
SOCCER
SHIP
MOMMY
AND POP
BOY
SUPER
EARTH
MATRIARCH
MUM
NATURE

Answer key for song lyrics and artists matching puzzle on page 21

Song Lyrics Just For Mom

1. Stacy's mom has got it going on. C

2. Mama, I love you, Mama I care. D

3. If daddy had only seen...mommy kissing Santa Claus last night! H

4. Hey Mama, I wanna scream so loud for you...Cuz' I'm so proud of you! I

5. Mama don't cry no more... better days are there for sure. B

6. I want a mom that will last forever; I want a mom who will love me whatever. G

7. Cuz' mom you were always there...the perfect fan. E

8. Momma, all you had to offer was the promise of a lifetime of love. K

9. Mom, her face is still the same, she never seems to change, her love will still remain. A

10. Mamma, Thank you for who I am. J

11. Mamma, woo-oo-oo-oo; didn't mean to make you cry. L

12. So, mother, I thank you, for all you've done and still do. F

13. Ain't nobody got a mom like mine. M

A. Earth, Wind and Fire

B. Gyptian

C. Fountain's of Wayne

D. The Spice Girls

E. Backstreet Boys

F. Christina Aguilera

G. Cindy Lauper

H. Jimmy Boyd

I. Kanye West

J. Il Divo

K. Celine Dion

L. Queen

M. Meghan Trainor

Ralph hopes you enjoyed his Mother's Day Gift Book. Don't forget the entire line of <u>Ralph Lane Gift Books</u> including:

<u>Dad Jokes Gift Book</u>
<u>Dad Jokes Christmas Gift Book</u>
<u>Dad Jokes Valentine's Day Gift Book</u>
<u>Dad Jokes St. Patrick's Day Gift Book</u>
<u>Dad Jokes Easter Gift Book</u>

Also consider buying Ralph's favorite book of all time:

<u>The Legend of Decimus Croome: A Halloween Carol</u>
available in paperback, Kindle and Audible formats.

Follow <u>Ralph Lane on Facebook</u>.

Made in the USA
Middletown, DE
06 May 2019